Maurice Thompson

The Ethics Of Literary Art

The Carew lectures for 1893, Hartford Theological Seminary

Maurice Thompson

The Ethics Of Literary Art
The Carew lectures for 1893, Hartford Theological Seminary

ISBN/EAN: 9783741199165

Manufactured in Europe, USA, Canada, Australia, Japa

Cover: Foto ©Andreas Hilbeck / pixelio.de

Manufactured and distributed by brebook publishing software
(www.brebook.com)

Maurice Thompson

The Ethics Of Literary Art

THE

ETHICS OF LITERARY ART

THE CAREW LECTURES
FOR 1893
HARTFORD THEOLOGICAL SEMINARY

BY

MAURICE THOMPSON

Author of "A Tallahassee Girl," "Sylvan Secrets,"
"Songs of Fair Weather," "Poems," etc.

❂

HARTFORD, CONN.
Hartford Seminary Press
1893

❊

THE matter of the following pages was delivered in three lectures, and it will not be hard for the reader to find the lines of division. A different plan might have been followed had my purpose originally been a book. Still I have not felt it necessary to recast any part of the work, and in arbitrarily dividing my discussion into three parts, it came easy to make Conception, Composition, and Expression stand, in the order named, as themes for successive treatment.

No careful reader will need to be told that my aim has been at suggestion, and that I have not hesitated to sacrifice the graces of diction in order to say with fewest words what might have been turned to excellent account in the way of mere literature.

My subject covers the whole field of morals ; for life and literature cannot be separated so as to say that what is vicious in life is harmlessly delectable in literature. We live life to enjoy it ; we make and read literature to enjoy it. In either case enjoyment is not necessarily a light matter. It is a serious matter *in the long run; for down the centuries we grow toward what most delights us.*

I do not regard ethics with a long face and a drooping lip. Right-doing is not such a doleful thing that we need groan and look as if God-forsaken at mention of it. Like all precious substances, honor comes high if we count as valuable what we have to give up for it. The little we own of it may be made to go a long ways if we do not care to buy any more. Most of us have enough to make us quite aware of what duty is.

I have considered chiefly imaginative literature in this discussion, and have assumed that my suggestions are sufficiently connected to form the skeleton of a theory, critical and philosophical, which may be filled out and clothed by the student.

M. T.

Sherwood Place,
      Crawfordsville, Indiana,
                  August, 1893.

THE ETHICS OF LITERARY ART

JOSEPH ADDISON undertook to define critical taste in literature, and called it "that faculty of the soul which discerns the beauties of an author with pleasure, and the imperfections with dislike." But what is the distinguishing mark between "beauties" and "imperfections"? If ethics is the "art of conduct," it steps in to suggest moral responsibility. Sir Philip Sidney, that flower of manhood, declared that the end of all earthly learning must be "virtuous action"; and that the chief function of art seemed to be the engendering of good impulses,— "it moveth one to do that which it doth teach." Certainly this moving power is our test of genius. But too often genius sets its face the wrong way, and then, if we are moved by

it, our impulse is toward evil. An attack upon
our sensibility is more dangerous than one upon
our mere intellectuality; the secret sources
of action, no matter what materialists may guess,
lie deeper than the brain. We may not find
the seat of moral pleasure in any particular
nerve-cell, dissect no matter how carefully.
Men of easy leisure can perhaps afford to enjoy
theories as a sort of luxuries, as the gourmand
enjoys his *pâté de foie gras;* but in active,
militant life most of us must crush facts
together, and knead them rapidly into available
forms of aliment for body and soul. And it
is a rule of Nature that what is good for the
body is good for the soul. Health in the
broadest sense is the state of happiness.
Ethics, therefore, has perfect health in view;
a sound pure body and a sound pure mind with
which to pursue the conduct of life. What
is good for the soul is good for the body.

I assume that human ethics is the perfection of selfishness — but the selfishness of
the perfect man who can see that the good

of all mankind is his good, and that the only way to do self the highest service is to serve the race. To accept individual happiness, a variable commodity measured by dispositions as different as persons, and make it the criterion, would be to embrace anarchy. The wholesome notion of right must be human, not personal.

If ethics broadly stated is the art of conduct, in our present discussion we shall find it to be the conduct of art. And if human happiness, in the highest sense, is the end of ethics, no one will doubt that the ethical end of art is the same. To please the most perfectly organized and most nobly refined human taste would be the aim of true art, as it is the ethical desire to have all mankind fitted to enjoy true art. In this view the ethical and the æsthetical lines coincide throughout.

Many persons nurse a remarkable fear of didactic art ; but these are not clear thinkers. All art is didactic, positively or negatively, and wields an influence by attraction or repulsion. Perhaps it would be better to say that

2

every form of art creation attracts us toward
or away from that equilibrium of good which
is the perfection of human conduct.

I note that certain critics, who in one
way or another are apologists for immoral
literature, seem fond of the phrase, "artistic
conscience." As if the artist must have a
conscience different from that of any other
good man! He is a coward who in any exi-
gency makes his own case a special one. The
moral responsibility of the artist offers no
secret and private avenues of confession and
avoidance, and if it does, a true man ought
to be too proud to use them. In literature,
as in every other sphere of human conduct, we
must have vast charity for the man, but no
charity for the man's evil. Proper critical appreciation of Shelley's poetry, for example, does
not involve any such reckless eulogy of Shelley's character as has been the recent vogue in
America and England. Charity covers faults,
but it never lies about them or excuses them.
Ethics draws no distinction between the wife-

murderer who cleans stables or keeps a dive,
and the wife-murderer who writes a "Prometheus
Unbound," or an "Ode to a Skylark." The
right of the aristocrat is not available as a
shield against the operation of moral responsibility. The glamour of genius cannot blind
the eyes of God.

It has ever been the function of evil to
progress by means of fascination, and this
fascination is loosely and mistakenly regarded
as pleasure or happiness. The thrill of the
unholy is mistaken for the calm and lofty
ecstasy of pure joy. Ethics does not recognize
the legitimacy of evil delights, come from what
source they may. The making of a poem
which appeals to base sympathies, no matter
how perfect the art, is as vile an act as though
it were vulgarly done in prose. Our conception
of the notion of art takes its color from the
surroundings we give to it. If we deny it an
ethical environment, we make the artist a
being specially privileged to do evil for art's
sake. Such a conception robs the creative

act of every connection with the sources of true conscience, and sets artistic results apart as excrescences on the substance of life. If the poet, for example, is an agent with power to affect the currents of human conduct, what law of nature exempts him from the common obligation to affect them in a way to do the greatest good to the greatest number? A ribald song may appeal to a vast audience; it may have a haunting melody; but is it justified?

It is in one of the plays of Aristophanes, "The Birds," that a nightingale sings and, as one of the listeners remarks, "makes the wilderness sweet with tender breath of music." Here is a conception of pure and wholesome art in the wilderness of life; it breathes a civilizing sweet round about. The Greeks called the Muses "the lamps of the earth," as if to make them guides to lead out of darkness; and this is the key-note of Greek art, the fine note of open illumination. Matthew Arnold denied to the Greeks that magic of genius which he found in the Celts; but what magic is more sure or more potent than this light direct, this surprise of sound and joyous conception? Mind, I do not here speak of subject-matter, nor of treatment, but of the conception of the function of art, — namely, to lead by the cord of delight.

Suddenly the question, Whither is the young mind led by unbridled "art for art's sake"? I freely grant full sway to the phrase, "a clean mind can cleanly contemplate evil"; but can a clean mind be delectated with what is unclean? Surely we may discern the distinction here suggested. Youth is the period of happiness and desire, and to youth art makes its most moving appeal. Take the novel, the most popular form of art, and you note that it is the young who read and are swayed by powerful fiction. The tremendous fascination of evil gives to an immoral novel an impetus in the grooves of commerce. Young people, even the purest of them, are curious to know what lies between the lids of a scarlet book.

A high ethical conception cannot license art
to generate such curiosity and then feed it.

But certain artists say that their business
is not to furnish food for babes.   Very well.
Is the adult liberated to delectate himself with
evil ?   By what ethical law can the distinction
be recognized ?   If art is a factor in the conduct of life, our conception of it must be that
it symbolizes an act of the collective human
body and expresses an aspiration.   In every
area of human action, except, as it would seem,
the field of fine art, we are required to avoid
evil aspirations and to shun the company of
vice and filth.   Even the crudest observation
and the most rudimentary experience of life
convince us that we must grow like what we
contemplate, and that intellectual associations
give color to the soul.   There are no more inti-
mate and subtile intellectual associations than
those effected through literature.   The man or
woman we meet in a book walks into our
sanctuary of character and writes maxims on its
walls.   If we are libertines in art, what are

we in the finest tissues of character? The conduct of the imagination is the chemistry of life. Physiological study leads more and more toward the conclusion that thought-habit largely influences what we may call nervous alimentation, and nothing is more certainly known than that character-quality depends upon the health of the nerve centers. It is therefore of ethical importance to study the connection between the development of art and the evolution of character.

One theory is that civilization shapes art to suit its changes. The other theory views art as a factor in developing civilization. A sound thinker who has read history and observed life will blend the two theories into a reciprocal one; but the ethical importance of art will be found in its influence in shaping conduct. Without this influence it is a mere efflorescence of life. To my mind genius loses its salient value when it takes the attitude of accident and poses as a mere *lusus naturæ*, like a gall-nut on an oak leaf, or a wart on

your hand.   I like to regard it as a healthy
fruit tree, bearing wholesome and invigorating
fruit; a perfect soul working consciously and
with conscience to delight and refine all other
souls.

And yet my conception of art does not
recognize obvious didactics, or accept the
limitations of any arbitrary system of morals.
The key to art is taste, and taste is the finest
secret of conduct.   Behind taste lies moral bias,
from which the initial impulse of every art
movement springs; for it is moral bias that
controls every conception of the form and the
function of art.   This bias gets into the air
of an age; it is miasm or ozone; it is a co-
efficient operating with conscience or inspiring
irresponsible revolt.   Now, the deepest reach
of art is to engender a right bias, so that good
taste shall become hereditary.   Says De Quin-
cey, "the writer is not summoned to convince,
but to persuade"; and Joubert adds, "it is not
enough that a work be good; it must be done
by a good author."   At the present moment

of history we seem to be hesitating whether or not, after all, literature shall be regarded as a mere mode of commercial motion. "The first value of a book," said a publisher, "is its salability." This is a conception which destroys every imaginable basis of conscience in literary life, unless we can make good books salable; for the publisher holds command.

Both church and state have tried to educate taste by means of legal censorship. The practice has been as futile as the principle is despicable. Indeed, the circulation of a bad book is always urged to the maximum by legal prohibition. Human perversity is an element in every problem of reform. A man told me that he never thirsted for whisky save when in a prohibition state. To reform conduct we must educate life. If a man is suffering from blood-poisoning, we do not cure him by local treatment ; we try to cleanse his whole system. Ethics must regard the collective body as one patient whose disease is constitutional. The quack doctor panders to a maudlin weakness

of chronic invalids.   So in art a certain school
of quacks, like Ibsen and Tolstoï, fatten upon
the liberality of hysterical souls.

Speaking of false critics, sturdy and right-
minded John Dryden said: "All that is dull,
insipid, languishing, and without sinews in a
poem they call an imitation of nature." In our
day the so-called realists answer to Dryden's
description.   They boast of holding up a mirror to nature; but they take care to give
preference always to ignoble nature.   They
never hold up their mirror to heroic nature.
Have you observed how, as a man becomes a
realist, he grows fond of being narrow and of
playing with small specialties?   Have you
thought out the secret force which controls
the movements of this so-called realism, and
always keeps its votaries sneering at heroic
life, while they revel in another sort of life,
which fitly to characterize here would be im-
proper?   I can tell you what that force is.
It is unbelief in ideal standards of human
aspiration, and it is impatient scorn of that

higher mode of thought which has given the
world all the greatest creations of imaginative
genius. It is a long cry from Homer and
Aeschylus and Shakespeare and Scott to Zola
and Ibsen and Tolstoï and Flaubert; but it is
exactly measured by the space between a voice
which utters the highest note of its time and
civilization, and one that utters the lowest. I
say that these modern realists utter the cry of
our civilization's lowest and most belated element; and they call it the cry of modern
science. But science has nothing to do with it.
Science never disports itself in the baleful light
of mere coarseness; nor does it choose dry or
commonplace investigations simply because
they are dry and commonplace. In its true
sphere science aims to lift us above mysteries.
The same may be said of all the great masters
of art; they lift us above the mire of degrading
things. True, we find coarseness amounting
to what is foul in all the ancient classics, and
even in Chaucer and Shakespeare; but we cannot take shelter behind these to cast forth upon

the world our own surplus of filth.   The custom
of critics is in charity to refer the obscenities of
old writers to the moral taste of the time.
Shall we credit our own civilization with an
appetency for the *Kreutzer Sonata, Leaves
of Grass,* and *Madame Bovary?*   Have we
moved no farther than this during these centuries of Christianity?

I know absolutely nothing about theology,
which is doubtless to be counted in reckoning
what I come to, and I frankly say that I could
not, to save me, tell the difference between one
creed and another; but I have it clearly in
mind that Christianity is responsible for our
civilization, and is the datum-line to which we
must refer in all our measurements.   Our
enlightenment may be imaginary, the gleam
of a myth, but it comes from the Star of
Bethlehem.

Every reader is aware that there exists
a certain strained relation between art and
moral responsibility.   The first impulse of
a solicitous parent is toward forbidding novels

and dramatic literature to his children. The
college and the pulpit wrestle with a giant
doubt in the matter of approving the current
conception of art. We all feel that the contemporary artistic influence is subtly opposed
to the ethical verities. We find that in fiction
and poetry we are hobnobbing with persons
with whom we could not in real life bear a
moment's interview. It is not so much the
scenes and characters chosen; we might regard
these, as in real life, with a deep regret ; but the
conception of art and its function represented by
such a choice of subject and treatment suggests
a vicious trend of life.

Matthew Arnold's theory of "sweetness and
light" may be a trifle flabby when put to the
average test of practical experience ; yet to
irradiate light and to instill sweetness can never
be amiss; this indeed seems to me the only
excuse for art. Culture must, however, have
its root nourished in a stronger soil than that
of mere amiability. Art should stand for more
than an expression of good-natured commentary

on current life, or of ill-natured caricature of humanity's frailties. "What is realism?" inquired a young woman the other day. Her friend answered, "It's writing what we are too clean to speak, and reading about what we would blush to look at. It is going in books where to go in actual life would disgrace us." Prudery does not appeal to a sound soul, and our strictures on art ought not to be different from our strictures on life. Our associations in art should not be lower than our associations in life. Indeed, to me the main service of imaginative activities is in giving higher experiences than ordinary life can afford. In life we aim at the higher life; in art, why not at the higher life? The most abject prudery is that which makes us ashamed to insist upon cleanness and soundness; the vilest dishonesty suggests that we account for literary villainy on the score of compulsion by "artistic conscience." Evil is the great foe of true happiness; but art must give canvas-room for this dark figure with all its scowls and all its fascinating smiles; it has a

mighty value when set over against goodness
to the effect that the conception holds fast to
the right. But let us not pass the limit of
freedom into the domain of license. In life
we face the ills and evils of our state; we
must do the same in art, and in both life and
art there must be moral responsibility. If in
writing a book we must not steal the thought-
work of a fellow, surely in the same pages
we must avoid breaking the other nine com-
mandments. Still I have known a man who
complained loud and long of the immorality of
a publisher who had failed to make accurate
copyright reports of sales in the matter of a
vilely impure novel. This is the special pleading which in another form demands that the
artist clothe himself before painting a naked
picture.

Plato's dreams and Aristotle's facts may
come at last into coincidence, and yet Plato's
conception is the only safe ground of art. An
imagination which never goes above "scientific
dissections" may state conditions; but a flash

of empyrean fire cuts through conditions and
illuminates the remote high area of the uncon-
ditional.   Plato's attitude was supremely artistic; Aristotle's posture was realistic.   The
utilitarian, who measures life by material units,
is a peripatetic ; the true artist is platonic, and
wherever we find him indicating an ethical conception, it is a universal one.   The old Dorian
notion was the elemental one, that morality was
not of the individual but of the people, and this
is the poet's notion in all ages.

But how is ethical leaven to work in literary
art ?   We cannot brook legal censorship, and,
if we could, the remedy would be worse than
the disease.   Freedom must be next to absolute
in letters.   The one feasible scheme of ethical
reform is education.   And   here   arises   the
abrupt question, By what particular channel of
education can literary taste be most readily
purified ?   It is safe to assume that a wholesome conception of art is the first stage of
reform needed, and I suggest that sound criticism would be a potent factor in the work; but

I speak of criticism in its most liberal sense, certainly not in the sense which would make the critic a mere friendly purveyor of appreciation, a sycophant self-trained to lick boots. The zealous fault-hunter, to be sure, is not a critic; no more is the fault-dodger. I like to read Sainte-Beuve; but I lay at his door and Wordsworth's much of the insignificance of literary art at this moment. The conception of art in the body of Wordsworth's poetry and the notion of criticism in Sainte-Beuve's essays have easily formed the whey of commonplace and the curd of "appreciation."

It is the habit of certain editors, I am told, to have their book reviews written by persons who will be sure to praise each work. This is but another expression of that irresponsibility behind which literary folk delight to huddle. The same weakness affects the whole modern theory of criticism. What avails teaching if in the same school every theory, no matter how debauching, has its expert apologist? If criticism is nothing more than sympathetic exposition by a special pleader, it amounts simply to the critic's saying: "I can make this artist's purpose and meaning plainer and more enjoyable than he could himself."

Criticism is the measuring of conduct — the conduct of life, the conduct of art. Viewed broadly, it is the fine residuum of sound morals left over after the solution of ethical problems. One man is not a critic; it is the intelligent majority. Say what we may, the average mind is the triumphant criterion; by it life wins or loses in all that concerns the body of humanity. What does not concern humanity as a body ought not to concern any man. We are the Adam and Eve of to-day; it is mankind that must make the long run, not the individual. If we suffer from the old Adam's fall, what countless millions must writhe far down the future because we, the new Adam, ate a more deadly fruit! Verily, the day is ours and the light of it.

It will be felt that I am suggesting immanent criticism, the floating, general, vital impression out of which the elusive but powerful influence of art is so largely drawn. What makes a book popular? No number of favorable reviews can do it — no amount of advertising or puffing. The secret lies in touching the nerve of average taste. Every proposition submitted to mankind is at last solved by this average immanent criticism. Artists may rebel; but the democracy of human economy always prevails, and that picture, that poem, that story which appeals to and satisfies a common and steadfast human longing is the lasting and influential one. Ethics, then, as it regards art, must respect the average, and the ethical aim must be to lift the line of mean human aspiration. To have no privileged class and to admit no special pleading in favor of genius by which strict moral responsibility may be avoided in art, are prerequisites of critical honesty. The average mind may be easily convinced of the justice of this democratic rule, and to this end should education tend. The higher we urge the mean level of immanent human criticism, the higher will rise the sur-

face of human conduct. The conduct of art
has no special exemption.

The chief office of art is to teach through
fascination, not openly and dictatorially, but
almost unawares. Its appeal is the charm of
beauty, the lure of symmetry, the perfume of
truth; or it is the imperious fascination of evil
clothed in a counterfeit divinity. This is the
old demarcation between good and evil. I
repeat that neither genius nor art can success-
fully slink out of responsibility through a
special side gate. To prevent this cowardice
the old Greeks invented dialectics and discussed
life vigorously in their schools. We may say
that they were heathens; but what would they
say of us with our Christian theories and our
pagan practices? Nakedness, physical and
spiritual, in art was a sincere reflex of Greek
religion, Greek civilization. It was uncon-
sciously projected. Not so with us; when we
go naked it is done self-consciously, with the
full understanding that nakedness is not decent.
We do it in sheer defiance of immanent criticism.

Is there a man or a woman in the world who believes that any person ever read a novel or a poem for the stark purpose of moral reform? Do you ever read a novel expecting thereby to wash away some stain from your character? Be honest and answer that in every quest pleasure is your goal. From the notion of heaven down to the wish for a tin whistle your aim is pleasure. You imagine you would enjoy heaven; you feel sure that a tin whistle would delight you. If you buy *Anna Karénina* or *Madame Bovary*, it is for delectation and not for personal purification. Speaking of cant, what cant is worse than that of the artist who entertains you at the table of vice with the avowed purpose of sweetening your life?

It is that wonderful Joubert again who says, "Naturally, the soul repeats to itself all that is beautiful or all that seems so." The writer writes what he likes, the reader reads what is to his taste. Ah, taste! there is the foundation. Can you for a moment credit any man's statement that he reads for delectation and yet

against his taste? Perhaps I am a Philistine;
at all events I do not hesitate here flatly
to charge insincerity. Who could possibly be
more hopelessly insincere than the avowedly
pure woman who tells you that she has fortified
her virtue by reading Ibsen's picture of Hedda
Gabler? Woman, you have taken Ibsen's arm
and have gone with him into vile company and
have been delighted with the novelty of it. The
smack of hell is sweet to your lips, as it was
to those of new-made Eve. It would be strictly
true for such a woman to say, "Yes, I read
these novels of impure passion, and there is
a strain in my taste which enjoys these
pictures of temptation and of evil pleasures.
Secretly I like a peep into debauchery; but
then I hold on to my own rectitude." The
word "rectitude" as here used means formal
rectitude of life's exterior; the intrinsic muscles
have responded to a coarse and beastly impulse.

In producing works of art having evil for
their source of fascination, and in reading such
works, we are tainting the most secret veins

of immanent criticism. Civilization inevitably responds to these influences working at the farthest tips of its tenderest roots. Vitiate imagination and you destroy character. No pure woman ever wrote a fiction of illicit love; if she began pure, she ended soiled. Her soul followed her pen. Druggists and physicians have told me that a person who takes to opium-eating will lie, steal, or barter body and soul for a morsel of dried poppy-juice. Never in my life have I known a man or a woman given over to the pleasure of writing or of reading novels based on illicit love who did not habitually lie to avoid the application of personal responsibility.

To the perfectly unbiased observer nothing is clearer than that forbidden fruit is always in demand, and will be as long as human perversity fortifies human animalism. If the author of *Tess of the D'Urbervilles* would say the truth, he would flatly confess that he wrote that brilliantly fascinating, filthy novel, not to make poor young girls cling to virtue, not to prevent rich young men from being villains at heart; but to make a fiction that would appeal to human perversity and delectate human animalism. He reckoned safely; the book sold almost as fast as whisky. It was named by the author "the story of a pure woman." This woman, after being easily led to shame once prior to marriage, fell again during wedlock, and then committed murder and was executed. This is no extreme case; I cite it as typical. Nearly all of the critics were loud in praise of this novel — thousands of good people read it. And to justify themselves both critics and readers claimed for it a high moral influence. What I see wrong in this is that it claims for fiction a power and an exemption not possible to real life. How can association with immoral and debauching people and conditions in our reading differ from our association with them in life? If art is chiefly for delectation, is it not a species of debauchery to indulge in art which takes its fascination from forbidden sources? As I have said, human perversity demands the forbidden. A publisher told me that for a novel to gain the reputation of being written in the highest strain of art and yet on a subject not considered clean was a sure guaranty of success ; "and yet," said he, "popular sentiment is strong against such books." Here is the fascination of the unclean — the very fascination which it is the duty of all to avoid and which it is the highest mission of Christian civilization to extinguish. And yet Christian artists demand the right to make commerce of this same evil fascination, and in this demand they are upheld by Christian critics.

In a word, I conclude this part of my argument by propounding a question, Has the immanent meaning of Christian civilization yet showed itself in art? Or, negatively, Is not fine art, and especially literary fine art, still essentially heathen? Is not the most direct and vigorous appeal of current poetry and fiction made to the ancient, elemental, conscienceless substance of humanity? One of

5

two things is certainly true, — the artist is specially exempt from moral responsibility, or he is just as responsible as any other person.

To me it appears that the commercial value of literary filth is really behind every argument in favor of the moral force assumed by authors and critics to be inherent in the dramatic presentation of illicit love. We must admit that novels and poems on this subject are immensely fascinating and that in a cold commercial view they are good property. In the same view whisky and gambling rooms are excellent investments. Gilded dives pay large dividends in the lawful currency. St. Peter's Church has fewer visitors than Monte Carlo. What do you make of this? Is it the true conception of art that the artist may live in honor by the same appeal which enriches the faro-dealer, the saloon-keeper, and the princess of a bagnio? Is the money earned by writing and selling *Tess of the D'Urbervilles* one whit cleaner than that earned by any other play upon the human weakness for unclean things?

It is not clear why a feeling should prevail that, to be robust, art must show a great deal of vulgarity. The best athlete carries but little flesh, and I find that fine muscles and sound nerves go farther than fat. Grossness, indeed, is as far removed from true virility as one pole from the other. Mere audacity in handling things not considered by the spirit of our civilization touchable cannot win the badge of Homer or of Horace. Homer sang strictly within the spirit of his age and voiced its characteristic aspiration. Horace did no violence to the civilization that inspired him. Full, close, sympathetic touch with Christianity (not with dry dogma, creed, ritual, or sect, or denomination), close touch with Christianity, I say, can give the only true conception of the new art of our just dawning era.

You will observe that I do not hesitate to speak of Christianity as distinct from church, priesthood, theology, and formal religion, — as a mode of progress, a great mood of civilization, broadening, deepening, warming day by day.

It is moving toward the republic in every-
thing; not backward toward the republic of
the heathen, but forward to the republic of
the Christian. Wherefore the conception of
art, to be adequate, must apprehend this future
while availing itself of the past. The point
where the old orb and the new blend the rays
of warning and of prophecy is the true focus of
inspiration. We must know where we are.
There is no return. The Greek with his
jocund heathen song is dead; gone is the
heathen grace of Virgil; gone the goatherd
genius from the fells of Sicily; gone Anacreon,
the ruddy bibber, and gone the strange cry:

> Ὦ παῖ παρθένιον βλέπων.

Not much less remote echoes the Dantesque
strain, half Christian, half heathen. It is time
for the key-note of our era to sound; it is
time for genius to speak in the true, in the
highest terms of our civilization.

"Well," says some practical soul, "when,
where, and to what purpose?" I answer:
When we make for genius the true Christian

atmosphere; in that atmosphere will he thrive;
not in the dust of dogma; not in the twilight
of cathedrals; not yet in the cramped sanctuary
of tradition. He shall inhale the rich air, which
is buoyant with the significance of our era, and
his purpose shall be the good of the brotherhood
of man.

In my remarks on the ethical conception of
literary art I have tried to suggest the alien
nature of the prevailing current criticism and
to refer it to the residual heathenism in our
civilization. You will pardon me if I am not
relying upon lightness of touch. An earnest
man addressing earnest souls need not avoid
direct expression in order to etherealize phrases.
I have assumed that a civilization generates immanent criticism to which that civilization's art
ought to conform in order to be æsthetically
and ethically adequate.

There are periods when this immanent criticism is smothered by factitious and alien forces.
The Alexandrine period in Greek poetry is a

typical one.   There art almost completely
divorced itself from the human soul and became
a mechanical exhibit.   A sound thinker would
expect this aberration of criticism to be attended
by a thoroughly artificial life as devoid as possible of sincerity.   Alexandria under Philadelphus
was a city of critics ; but then, as now, the
critic's chief concern was to do something call-
ing attention to himself.   The richness of the
Ptolemæan civilization was wasted on mere form
which really expressed nothing.   What I will
call the sense of composition, the artistic consciousness of an organism to be spoken into life
by genius, was dormant.   At the great school
of Philadelphus phraseology counted for every-
thing ; a living form of art-creation was not
thought of.   Even Theocritus, the one "burning mouth of the muses" in that artificial day,
lost his sense of composition at the gate by
which he entered Alexandria.

Before then the Greeks had formed their art
on free lines guided by the spirit of their
religion.   What the word "freshness" best inti-

mates hung upon their thoughts like a dew of morning. You can discover nothing alien to Greek civilization in Homer or Pindar or in the fragments of Anakreon and Sappho. Those poets were guided by the immanent criticism of their times, and so they voiced absolute sincerity. If you will read the seventh Idyl of Theocritus, you will be aware of a certain something, like a fruit-zest or a root-pungence, which, when you analyze it, seems composite, a mingling of many ancient savors and fragrances. Here is native honey brewed directly from the innermost nectaries of a civilization. The happy Greek had not yet remodeled the syrinx of Pan to suit the artificial music of Alexandria. I would accept this Thalysia by Theocritus as a singularly apt illustration of the limiting influence exerted by academical criticism. At the time of its writing Theocritus had just reached manhood and while yet fresh from bathing long and deep in the Pierian spring of old Greek religion was just at the margin of that African desert called the Alexandrian school.

After that idyl he wrote nothing of real value
because he quit the field of true artistic conscience and went to pose for favor in the eyes
of incest while studying the forms of a conventional artisanship.   Plainly he was eager to
barter conscience for gold; and for success in
literature he would gladly part with every trace
of original freshness and independence.

With the apostacy of Theocritus, Greek
genius came down from the slopes of Helicon
and merged itself for ever in the commonplace.
What Alexandrine influence was to Greek
literature the so-called realistic influence is to
the literature of to-day.   We might aptly call it
literary dry rot.   There is no doubting the
Alexandrine attitude.   While exalting Homer
and Aeschylus, as we do Scott and Shakespeare, they assumed to command a finer art
than those old masters ever knew.   So the
other day a leading realist boldly affirmed the
art of his own contemporary school to be finer
than that of Scott, Thackeray, and Dickens.
There was the smack of Callimachus and

Philetas in such a morsel of criticism. Callimachus, you know, set himself up for a critic of
Homer, and, after attempting epic production
and failing, came to the conclusion that it was
a finer art than Homer's to write an ode to a
woman's hair. To-day the prevailing criticism
seems to be that to surpass Shakespeare in
drama, and Scott in novel-writing, one has but
to present commonplace life with the clever
touch of conventional humor.

We of the Western world have accepted
realism and suited it to an Abderian mood ; we
have laughed it into a sort of popularity as a
fun-bundle, and have made believe that we cannot comprehend the difference between art and
photography — between the divine verisimilitude of a work of genius and the mere poll-
parrot reporting of clever note-takers in fiction
and poetry. It amuses us to be bored. In this
temper, content to laugh at ourselves, we are
making little progress in serious art. So,
when the conscientious critic comes to look
facts in the face, he is surprised at the poverty

6

of our genius in composition. We have sketches, studies, bits of local color, broad dashes of caricature ; but very little that fills the measure of original composition full and finished. What appears to me to be the cause of this is a deep-seated misapprehension of ourselves as a people. We are too sure that it would be well for us to be English, or Russian, or French, instead of being American ; but our social morals are not yet bad enough to admit of the alien treatment, wherefore most of our art has a foreign subject or is at least international to let in the filth.

Composition in art comprehends substance and structure. The true artist designs no lifeless image ; he creates an organism informed with the spirit of a strong aspiration. It is safe to add that every true creation of genius is immortal, immortally good or immortally bad in the broadest ethical sense. As an organism its natural habitat is Hell or Heaven, its influence benign or malignant. The sanest and wisest among us may fancy that to read a romance like *Manon Lescaut* or a novel like *Madame Bovary*, and discreetly admire its art is not so bad; but in applying the high calculus of ethics and passing to the limit of moral responsibility, what difference appears between the encouragement of such art and the encouragement of any other evil communication to the imagination of mankind? Some one says that evil must go into art. So it must. It has its important place in composition. Immanent criticism makes us aware of this. What Emerson called "the burden of the Bible old" assigns it a large area and suggests its function in every poem, every drama, every romance based upon human nature and human experience or aspiration. Well does the philosopher of Concord remark that belief in immortality would necessarily take "a base form for the savage and a pure form for the wise." The distinction is just as clear in art. A gross or unwise taste naturally gives evil preference to good in making an article to delectate imagination withal. Here is the secret and here is the menace against

which we cast ourselves.   To set good and evil
over against each other in art, preserving their
true ethical relations and comparing them without prejudice, is the office of composition.
Even "art for art's sake," of which our eyes and
ears have long been weary, finds nothing in
imagination to justify weaving a lure whereby
to lead pure beauty into the mire of unholy
places.   Such a sacrifice is always made on the
altar of a sordid god.

A word here on "sensational" composition.
Critics are not very clear in applying the ad-
jective "sensational."   Some harmless and
even valuable romance has to bear that name,
while the vilest of French intrigue betinseled
with what is called "realistic faithfulness to
truth" meets with unqualified critical approval.
Passing to the most violent extreme, let a sound
conscience decide between the "dime dreadful"
and *Tess of the D'Urbervilles* on the score of
subtile and deep sensational energy.   On your
honor, if compelled to decide, which would you
prefer, that your boy should read *Dick Dead-*

shot and dream of being a bold rider among the cows, or that your daughter should pore over the temptations of *Tess* till every handsome young man she saw looked to her like a leering *roué* in polite disguise? It is composition, not diction that makes a work sensational.

It is the choice of figures and the determination of their attitudes and meaning individually and collectively that impresses the imagination, and somehow what is named realistic fiction always leaves the autograph of pessimism on the reader's heart. In the end everybody comes to actual or constructive grief and the few who deserve well usually have the worst of the bargain. Whether it is a government, a sermon, a machine, a poem, or a novel, composition fixes the equilibrium and so controls the scope of influence. A prize-fight is a drama as complete as *Hamlet* or *Ivanhoe ;* but in the prize-fight we have only the rudimentary composition of absolutely savage taste. At the other extreme we have the refined, emasculate art of Flaubert and Guy de Maupassant.

Was it Sophocles who said that Aeschylus "did right, all unaware of it"? It is much easier to reach the other habit and do wrong by mere momentum of acquired conditions. This is true of nations, as of individuals; and we shall find the composition of political life, the arrangement and emphasis of its masses and the significance of its groups and figures sympathetically if not directly connected with the source of imaginative inspiration and controlled by the prevailing popular dream. If you will observe the composition of the French government under the last Napoleon, its likeness to that of Flaubert's and De Maupassant's novels will strike you with startling force. Rottenness of substance and of meaning—debauchery, opium and absinthe, utter absence of conscience, pyæmia, softening of the brain, suicide or the mad-house; these attend the composition wherein evil predominates.

It may seem to you that I am not saying much about ethics as a science. There is no such science. Do right. But where dwells the science of it? Shall the pot say to the kettle, "thou art black," or the diamond to the dew-drop, "my light is the only"? Behind diamond and dew-drop is the sun, and behind blackness is the source of it. Neither force to drive nor laws to prohibit can bring about the conditions favored by ethics. The fiber, the tissue, nay, the very nerve-fluid of the social body, is to be reached and educated by sweet persuasion applied to that strange source of all human progress, the imagination. Compulsion breeds perverse stubbornness; prohibition develops unquenchable desire for the forbidden fruit. This was the springe in Eden. The moment that man shall enact a law of ethics, woe be to the heretics! We shall then feel again how the axe, the fagot-fire, and the thumb-screws can establish the inviolability of a creed, the inerrancy of a text. We hear much about "higher criticism." Let us have it all along the line; it may be a "fad," it may be a revelation; it is death to esoteric bigotry. Do you imagine that truth will wither under the directest and whitest ray of this higher criticism ? Analysis does not affect ethics in any way ; truth is a single and simple substance, absolutely pure and indestructible.

Be sure of one thing : the immanent power of Christian civilization is freedom of investiga-gation and nothing which shrinks from the severest test will long appeal to credence. The stupendous composition called Greek mytho-logy or Greek religion would be a living or-ganism to-day had it been true in the first place. The higher criticism dissolved it because it was not a truth. The grip of vitality is fastened in the roots below every possible reading and re-vision. The composition, the attitude of groups and masses, the composite whole, invite belief or disbelief. We are a Christian people because the composition of the Christian picture has met our approval. The moment that an arbi-trary edict sets the picture aside as specially ex-empt from critical tests, that moment a smile and a wink of doubt disturb the face of Chris-tendom. It looks too much like a precaution against the dissolution of another mythology. The old way of enforcing educational measures was with a rod. Now we appeal, not by brute force, but by tender kindness. Not so long ago witches were burned a few miles from here, and just over yonder the Protestant felt fire and thumb-screw. To-day is the day of open freedom, and the difference must be respected. But education must not in the name of freedom assume license. The only safe taste is that grounded in the deepest meaning of our civilization. To me the word " heresy " is not a pleasing one; it brings to my ears the hissing of flames, to my nostrils the smell of burning human flesh. I like better the word " education," and I delight in coupling it with freedom and light. Search the Scriptures of all ages and all peoples ; eternal life is visible by eternal light. Shut off one ray from the picture and the composition is blurred.

The finest quality of a composition is authenticity, which shows it steadfast after all mutations of time, manners, and creeds. Such

7

a composition is a criterion only so long as it can resist the criticism of all comers; its inerrancy must meet and vanquish every new era's suggestion of readjustment, else suspicion will eat against it like an acid. Not all the critics and grammarians of the Alexandrine period could dim one flower of Homer. What "higher criticism" is likely to shake the solid pillars of the Bible? With every failure of the critic to remove the foundations of divinely inspired authority, the Book of Books takes deeper hold upon human credence and shows the more its solidity. So it is with the humanly inspired works of art. We put them to the test of higher criticism, and if they stand we know that their value is not a moment's accident or the result of a mere factitious vogue. It may be that some Callimachus of to-day dreams that Scott's day is over; but the vitality of organic composition keeps and will keep those grand romances alive. The groups and masses of history are there; the significance of true manhood and womanhood is there; the appeal of honor and courage is there, and life is there bearing itself heroically. Everybody loves a hero.

The fascination of a composition is always romance ; good or evil it is still romance. Your sermon, your picture, your house, your novel, your poem, your religion, must satisfy the imagination with romance. Romance is not a lie ; it is the surprise of the picturesque. Call up Adam and Eve, or Romeo and Juliet, and there is the composition of romance. Come reverently and with unfaltering credence to the story of Christ's life and death, and tell me truly, did Aeschylus, did Shakespeare ever write so picturesque a tragedy ? When you tell that story to your child, it clutches his imagination and holds it fast. The wonder of it comes before any deeper significance is comprehended. Here lies the secret of imaginative appeal whether the composition be of life or of fiction. Beecher, Phillips, Webster, and Emerson knew it and used it in sermon, oration, lecture. Napoleon the First, Hugo, Scott, Shakespeare, Plato, Aes-

chylus, Sappho felt its imperious power. Begin
in the far mist of antiquity and come down to
the present with microscopic scrutiny, and you
cannot lay hand on any great achievement
which had not its hero and its romance.

You academic men are fond of invoking the
"scientific spirit." Well, invoke it now. Col-
lect the facts of literary history, mass them,
classify them, analyze them, and then show
me one, just one immortal work of fiction,
drama, oratory, or poetry, or religion which
has not romance as its chief source of appeal. Throw in history for good measure,
and still the rule holds. Heroism, extraordinary
events, the roll and crash of war, great reforms,
the villainies of tyrants, the divine patience of
saints, the influence of beautiful women, the
charm of poets, the building of temples, the de-
struction of cities, wonderful discoveries and in-
ventions, revolutions in religion and philosophy,
—take these from history and who will read
or remember it? Take any period of our
country's life and eliminate the extraordinary

features, the pioneers, the heroism of '76, the mediæval romance of slavery, the great war, Washington, Lincoln, Grant, Lee, Beecher, Whittier, Stonewall Jackson, Ossawattomie Brown, Grover Cleveland, the ocean telegraph, the stupendous growth of wealth and liberal education, — take out the extraordinary and you have no book to write of us. Or if you should persist and write the book it would have no significance, no human appeal. Take the extraordinary from science and what is it?

Do you understand how Darwin's theory took hold of mankind? Do you fancy that it captivated a mere "scientific" taste? Not that. Never did human imagination find a more wonderful romance than this story of the origin of species and the descent of man. Agnostics like to smile at the simple Bible story of creation as at a nursery tale. Well, the story may not be literally true, it may not be true at all; but this romance of evolution, is it literally true? Is it true at all? Go ask the sphinx if its ancestors knew. Like a child with a new toy, the human imagination plays with "natural selection" and "the survival of the fittest," and for a little while is content. For awhile it is Darwin ; yesterday it was Humboldt or La Place ; the day before it was Pythagoras. Always it is the genius who presents a great romantic composition. Darwin's theory may be true; it may be false ; but it is extraordinary; it is picturesque, and it appeals to the elemental universal love of the wonderful in the human mind. When Leibnitz and Newton were discovering calculus imagination was on tip-toe to catch the first glimpse of infinity.

If you plan to control men, you first captivate their imagination. Give me the key to a people's imagination and you may have the rest; I will lead them through nine crusades in spite of you. Peter the Hermit, John Law, Napoleon, Pasteur, old John Brown — every man who has shaken the world did it with the lever of imagination. When lately the curtain was wrung up and Doctor Pasteur made his bow we were for a thrilling moment sure that

there stood the master of disease and death.
The light of perennial health flashed from continent to continent. To-morrow some other
great romancer of science will arise. We shall
turn our backs upon the epic of microbes and
hang Pasteur's picture in the garret with those
of Descartes, La Place, and Buffon. It all
comes to one goal, which every creative genius
grazes with the wheel of his chariot.

Eliminate from religion, any religion, its
specific romance, and you still have left the
ancient generic wonder of it. Take this away
and the residual composition will not attract a
second glance from mankind. Creeds are at
best but persistent, refractory wounds upon the
fair body of religion; mayhap some sweet day
they will all coalesce and heal without a scar.
But deprive religion of its vital romance and observe how quickly it dies. If we can rid our
minds of factitious reverence and give ourselves
over to true reverence, we shall for the first
time feel how God, the universe, religion, and
duty form in the imagination a picture sphered

on the radius of supreme beauty and harmony.
How petty and trifling a religion becomes the
moment it disengages itself, as Greek religion
at last did, from that highest credulity which
alone amounts to absolute faith, the credulity of
the imagination! What the human soul longs
for is the step beyond, the higher lift, the supreme surprise. Ethics enters the field to demand that this step beyond shall not be into the
pit, that this higher lift shall not be to the
mountain-top of temptation, that this supreme
surprise shall not come of evil splendor. It re-
quires that every scene of art shall be so com-
posed as to have its focus in a cleanly and
wholesome truth.

It has been well said that the novel is to-day
the most popular form of art; its composition
is a matter of large moment if it is come to be
an accepted factor in popular education. If it
is a physiological fact that imagination is the
chemistry of character, then the impression of a
composition addressed directly to the imagination may work profound evil or great good to

character. Bad as the French people are in some directions, they go farther than we do in protecting young girls from the danger of promiscuous fiction-reading. But I submit that if fiction is for education, it is for the young, it is for the formative period of life. To my mind the fact that a novel is unfit for open reading at the family fireside is positive proof that it is not wholesome reading for any person at any place.

Let us not lose sight of a very important distinction. Art is for delectation mainly, for moral teaching incidentally or unawares. Various useful studies are necessarily unfit for fireside rehearsal; yet they must be pursued. Not so with art; it is for the galleries of pure culture, for the walls of the churches and schools, for the home library, for the space over ·the library mantel. Let me say to you that certain assumptions of adults are known by young persons to be downright lies. For instance, when the father and mother of a bright, inquisitive family of children assume that Zola is delicious to old folk, bracing and

8

invigorating, but deadly to the souls of the young ! I have seen a father sneak away from his sons to take whisky before breakfast. I have seen a legislator blowing cigarette smoke through his own nose while framing a law to prohibit the sale of cigarettes to young men. The prohibition was all right, but the assumption was a lie. A vice is not to be thus suppressed. While you sit at the head of the table quaffing *Manon Lescaut* and *Tess* and *Anna Karénina* and *Kreutzer Sonata*, your children know what flavor it is that you like. You may tell them that you sip those tipples for the good of your mature soul ; but they will know that you are a mature prevaricator. The least sophisticated mind in all the world is not deceived when it reads an immoral novel which pretends to have a moral purpose, nor can you hoodwink even a babe by pretending that you read such a novel with a view to purifying your own morals.

It seems to me that æsthetics and pessimism cannot blend together; therefore true art is nec-

essarily optimistic. Even tragedy must offset
its catastrophe with a glimpse of eternal justice,
or it must leave a bad shadow in the mind.
What you read is a personal experience to you.
If you read pessimism with delight, your imagination makes you a pessimist. Glance at the
sublime master-tragedy of all time and the comfort of the resurrection redeems it from pessimism. Leave Christ a dead preacher between
two dead thieves, and you rob the tragedy of its
most precious human appeal. Giotto stabbed a
man to death in order to paint Christ's death-
agony. Realism could go no further; for the
resurrection does not appeal to it. A composition need not be a sermon when it is called a
poem or novel; but it must not meanly dodge
being one. I heard a man curse like a pirate to
remove a suspicion that he was a preacher.
Some novelists seem to go far aside to make
their stories unquestionably devoid of every
evidence of moral responsibility or ethical significance. Others distort their compositions
with maudlin sentimentalities, thinking by this

means to prove their loyalty to the sweet
springs of human kindness. In the conduct of
life neither these nor those are of good account.
A faithful, authentic composition addressed to
our Christian civilization should have its masses
balanced so that the main aspirations of that
civilization are clearly acknowledged. Spontaneous, native art never fails in this. The un-
erring Greek artist rooted every drama, every
lyric, every dream of sculpture in the soil
where the flowers of his religion grew. I do
not mean that art must be religious ; I admit
that if consciously religious it is likely to be
downright insipid ; but the immanent virtue of
a Christian civilization ought not to be absent
from its art.

I call serious attention to the indissoluble
connection between romance and religion, not
to belittle religion or to make irreverent com-
parison. Pure romance demands faith in the
largest possibilities ; religion exacts precisely
the same ; and if you will scrape off the veneer
of realism which scouts at romance, you will

find the substance of agnosticism. If you are
an agnostic, you are a realist; if you are a romancer, you have a religion. Religion appeals
to us for heroism. The oriental wife must burn
herself; the Mohammedan must fast forty days;
Gautama must agonize seven times seven days
and nights under the Bo-tree; Christ must
forego the luxury of worldly triumph to die a
felon's death for the good of mankind. But the
realists tell you that heroism like Christ's is sensational and in very bad taste.

One dreads to appear polemical; but how is
the issue here presented to be avoided? The
very criticism which cries, "Sensational! sensational!" against harmless melodrama, turns fond
and loving praise upon the *Sapho* of Daudet,
or *Tess* of Hardy. It seems that a heroic gen-
tleman or lady is a sensational figure; but a
heroic *roué* or extraordinary harlot falls naturally
into the composition of "high art!" We are
warned by these critics to avoid the unusual and
the extraordinary; but what is the usual and the
ordinary? Is it usual and ordinary for a girl to

be like "Daisy Miller" on one hand, and like
"Tess" on the other? Which of these two is
the ordinary girl? One is the extreme of mil-
linery flimsiness, the other the extreme of dis-
honor. One is tinseled vulgarity, the other is
sainted debauchery; you pay your money and
take your choice.

Organized Christianity, using the phrase lib-
erally, ought to be the source of ethics in our
civilization; that is, it should be able to set the
pace of human conduct and give direction to
culture. It should be able to establish the general criterion by which to measure art. If it
cannot do this it must be radically defective as
a model composition. If it cannot hold, mould,
and color human imagination, its end is near.

Here is my scholium, Immanent criticism
is what a civilization thinks of itself. Whenever the written or unwritten constitution of
civilization loses its command of absolute credence, it fails. To command absolute credence
it must show itself absolutely invulnerable, at
least absolutely self-respecting. But what, in-

deed, does a civilization think of itself, what immanent criticism does it secretly, if not openly, generate by arbitrarily setting its constitution above the reach of free, honest, earnest, inexorable tests? You lose self-respect the moment that you claim special exemption from self-inspection or from public scrutiny.

But what has all this to do with the ethics of art? Look back into history and see. The composition of religion is the composition of art. The two are not identical; but they are, in a pure state, mathematically similar. The moment that the ancient religion of Greece tottered, its art tottered correspondingly. When the Pope was infallible Roman art was infallible. Whenever Christianity shall become homogeneous, when it shall not call honest investigation heresy, when it shall stand triumphantly inviting all tests, extrinsic and intrinsic, we may expect to see it set its ethical standard on the temple of life and the temple of art. But the cord of a creed drawn over-tight can strangle what it was noosed to save.

Let me earnestly disclaim any application of my remarks beyond the strict periphery of my subject. Let every word go straight to the relation of Christian ethics to the conduct of art. Creeds are good or bad; men multiply them at need; art has nothing to do with them, nor with the quarrels they engender; but it would seem that the ancient well-spring of our Christian civilization, if pure, as I believe it is, need fear no analysis of its water. And then, if the conduct of life, which is the subject of Christian ethics, has the correlation with the conduct of art which I have suggested, it is impossible to exaggerate the significance of recent movements of Christian thought when we would attempt to ascertain the effect upon both life and art of the critical standard likely to be established. The world is moving; it must move or die. Movement is life; stillness is death. Movement is reform; inertia is decay. The supreme composition of the universe tells us of a goal far beyond our vision. We must not struggle to prevent the waste of old tissues; for it is by such

waste that we live and grow. Each day we
must throw off error once thought to be truth.
This is the winnowing and selecting process of
progressive enlightment. What is the conclusion ? It is that, if ours is really a Christian
civilization, the controlling spirit of Christianity
ought to appear in its art composition ; that the
immanent criticism generated by Christianity
must in the long run shape the history of our
civilization, and in the long run Christianity
must bear the blame of our failure or the praise
of our triumph.

The Greeks had a word which perfectly ex-
pressed style, the word $\mathring{\eta}\theta o\varsigma$, which I would
translate by the phrase "smile of meaning."
The $\mathring{\eta}\theta\eta$ were the character-beams of a countenance, as if the soul looked out with a twinkle
of its own. They had another golden word,
$\theta\alpha\lambda\epsilon\rho\acute{o}\nu$, the bloom of vigor. If we could blend
the two words into one, it would give what I
want. Individuality, luminosity, sincerity, and
rosy health must characterize the expression of

9

sound art. Physicians say that our diseases register themselves in our faces; a disease of culture comes out in the lineaments of civilization. A sick man is whimsical; sick society indulges in 'fads;' to-day it cries for Tolstoï, to-morrow it whines for Ibsen.

A perfectly healthy civilization is a happy organism content with its natural bill of fare; and it remains healthy just so long as it holds to the soil of nativity and dreams not of alien manners. Such a civilization was the Greek; not merely conservative, but true to itself and sincerely homogeneous. Its religion turned out to be false, as any religion possibly may; still Greek sincerity and loyalty in religion was the standard of a perfect art. The Greek poet was a healthy animal, well-fed and well-groomed. In the light of his time he was good. He was a consistent and sincere heathen glad to be alive; his song was the perfect exponent of his nature. This reaching down to the original elements of character for the terms of expression justifies Buffon's definition, *le style est l'homme même.*

Style, when sincere, is civilization itself, and properly speaking there can be no such thing as insincere style. What we are apt to call style, in the literature of to-day, stands for nothing, being a mere whiff of evanescence puffed from the lips of conventional humor or stereotyped smartness ; it is not the spontaneous exhalation of elemental significance. It is interesting to observe how the self-styled realists go about trying to draw style out by connecting themselves with vulgarity, evidently mistaking it for simplicity. A vulgar spirit may be simple ; oftenest it is not ; true simplicity has a refining power which eludes academical control. Your simple man is clean, and he seems not to know it ; or at least makes no distinction of it. Your vulgar man, if not rank, has faith in the efficacy of low means. An old mountaineer doctor was called by a city woman touring in the hills to see her child, who was ill. "Madam," he said, "let yer little gal run out doors an' git some dirt. Gross personal cleanliness air very on-healthy." He was a critic laying down a maxim of realism. Another saying of his was: "A leetle bit o' clean dirt air not nasty." In other words a certain amount of filth is supposed to be necessary to vigorous life. I think that this notion as applied to literary art comes of a superficial reading of Chaucer, Shakespeare, Horace, Homer, and other old masters, and of mistaking their smut for their style.

It is past the time when a man can live like Diogenes or sing like Anakreon. A tub is no longer habitable, and our wine gives headache instead of joy. We should feel like very benighted children if we shaped our destiny by the direction of the Sybilline Books. It is the difference of civilizations that sets up the bar — it is the failure to take this difference into account that brings the realist to grief with his boasted sincerity. These realists forget, or mayhap never knew, that what superficially appears to be the most daring realism in Greek art was indeed the romantic flower of their religion and not a "society report" or a transcript of observation. What manner of impression of our era, its stupendous forces and its almost unimaginable significance will the far-off future man draw from reading one of Henry James's novels or one of Walt Whitman's poems? I do not speak of these two men as imitators; they are not that. What I do mean is that they do not see or express any of the deep character-lines of our civilization as a whole. What they grasp is exotic and superficial; each has imported his art-spirit, one from modern, artificial Europe, the other from ancient Egypt. One is infinitely crude, the other infinitessimally fine; neither expresses anything deeply characteristic of our civilization. Indeed, whenever we try to fit old life to a new body we always somehow get nothing but the dregs. Imitation invariably means the imitation of faults. It is said that in counterfeit money the simplest and clearest lines of engraving are most often badly executed. The same is true in counterfeit literature; we detect its spuriousness in the failure to reproduce authentic strokes.

To give composition the $\eta\theta o\varsigma$, the counten-

ance of character, and the θαλερόν, the clean,
fair bloom of vigor, is the highest function of
artistic expression. Those writers who have
most signally failed in expression have been
clearly wanting in this magnetism of literary
countenance. Walt Whitman pleases one reader
and repels ten thousand. Not so with Newman,
or Tennyson, or Robert Louis Stevenson, or
Nathaniel Hawthorne, or Lowell, or Howells.
These have the eye of the Ancient Mariner to
hold ten thousand, to repel none. With this
particular fascination the writer's subject-matter has nothing to do. He will detain you an
hour on your way to dinner with the analysis of
a vague smile just as easily as with an epic.

There are two extremes of artificial sincerity. Walt Whitman stands at one, the
" goody-goody " school at the other. You
know at a glance that Walt Whitman's sincerity is a matter of his own manufacture ; it is
an assumption that has grown into his tissues
and become indurated. So of the Sunday-
school story-writer. We all know that this his-

tory of the good little girl who came to be so sentimentally religious that she melted away into a sort of pathetic treacle for angel-bread is out of the bounds of all honesty. It is the worst of all sensational trickery. I count it the meanest of pessimism to make a child believe that the road to Heaven is always out of repair and its bridges broken.

Plato taught that pleasure is the return to nature; but the admirers of Walt Whitman accept no return to nature save that which brings up at brutal coarseness or even obscenity. Ethics demands a return to the divine purity, candor, and jocund optimism of nature. For without trust in the good of nature there is no ethics. If, as the realists represent, life is a failure and all of its stories come out wrong, how can conduct avail? You know that realists consider it maudlin art to have a novel end happily. When I hear a singularly emasculate literary voice prating about "inexorable art" and "merciless truth" I know that there's another disagreeable novel coming. Singularly enough,

but naturally, too, by the way, pessimism of conception and of composition has enforced ultra-
refinement of literary artisanship; for human
nature must have beauty, if not of substance,
then of surface.   What realism, so-called, lacks
in intrinsic interest is hoped to be compensated
for by extrinsic cleverness.   Mr. Howells must
have meant this when he said that in our day
literary art is finer than it was in the day of Sir
Walter Scott.   He meant a finer verbal artisanship; for who could believe that *Daisy Miller*
is a greater novel than *Ivanhoe?* The distinction to be drawn is between contents and
superficies.   We galvanize more cleverly than
Scott did; but do we equal the body of his art?

I have said that true expression is from
within, the exhalation or irradiation of meaning
and influence, the ἦθος and the θαλερόν of art.
No superficial dressing can give it; for it is not
like the sheen of varnish; it beams out from the
sphere's center and makes every substance a
fire-hearted crystal.   No amount of word-study
or of phrase-practice can compass style.   Dic-

tion may be perfected so that correct and flexible language becomes habitual; but the magnetism of expression is not to be drawn from grammar, or rhetoric, or dictionary. Here again comes in that subtile chemistry of character — imagination. There must be a clearly assignable difference between a pure and fine academical diction, and what we would mean by the phrase "a fascinating style." Something like far and fair perspectives glimpsed between words gives the sweet, strong sense of surprise, the precious shock of discovery, the unexpected return to nature.

Style is not literary, not bookish, not lubricated with lamp-oil and garnished with quotations and references, nor spiked with mere novelties. You find it as you find youth and beauty and rare charm of soul, quite free of debt to any loan-office and standing upon no patent of conventional nobility. It is by a writer's style that we get into his soul and breathe his moral atmosphere. Here the refined essence of his nature floats free, and here is distilled the dew of

10

his character.   So the highest personal compli-
ment we can pay an author is to tell him that he
has rare charm of style.   But what if he uses this
charm in the bazars of art to make poison-pro-
ducts look wholesome?   All along as we plow
our furrow of inquiry we turn up this stubborn
bulb of responsibility.   To the average tongue
it has an acrid taste, but we must bite it every
day and every hour of our toil, whether we
relish it or not.   Is it worth while to try to
imagine that in art there is a domain where the
love of evil brings no sense of ethical disturb-
ance?   The ill-starred men of genius have been
those who attempted revolt and tried to smother
the still, small voice in a wet blanket which they
called freedom.   The Villons, the Baudelaires,
the Byrons, the Rousseaus, the Shelleys, the De
Maupassants, all these, say what we may, looked
at good with a sinister eye of intense selfishness
and hate ; but they each gnawed a file.   These
anarchists in art are also antinomians in morals.
Not one of them ever drew a clean breath or
ever honored wedlock, wifehood, motherhood, or

womanhood, or virtue. They prated, with the thrilling power of genius, about freedom and conscience ; but what did they mean ? The up-shot of it all was they desired license. Villon desired to steal, Shelley wished to put away his wife and get another, Byron longed to be a libertine and yet be a hero. Now, at least two or three of these had great genius ; Shelley and Villon especially set a lasting fascination in their works, and although Byron does not wear so well, he compels a slowly relaxing attention as he retreats in the romantic distance. Rousseau's five children are still crying in the found-ling hospital and wondering what is the matter with the " Social Contract."

I am not appealing to the *argumentum ad hominem ;* I am suggesting the ἦθος, the char-acter-glow of these exponents of revolt against the inevitable good and of apology for the im-mitigable bad. From the heart's fullness the mouth speaketh. Here is anarchic liberty urged and merged into hideous personal license, and all so alluringly expressed that any restraint

seems a tyranny.   But it would be safe to say
that immanent criticism has settled the ethical
point in the light of our civilization.   Rousseau
made a revolution, and yet his books have not
kept their hold like those of Scott.   Sound-
hearted and true-souled Sir Walter speaks a
language informed with robust health and fra-
grant of moral purity and sanity.   We feel without going into biography that he has never de-
serted a wife or his children, or tried to upset
the laws of marriage.   He seems large, strong,
safe, steadfast; and we like to have him near
us.   An influence like his never leaves a morbid
heat in the nerve-centers, never suggests that
hell has some advantages over Heaven as a high-
toned summer resort.   After reading *Ivanhoe*
you may indulge some romantic desire for a
spear, a shield, an armored horse, and plenty of
muscle ; but you breathe good air and feel clean.
Not so at the end of a novel by Zola.   As
was said by a reader of Balzac, the first impulse
after laying aside one of his books is to wash
one's hands and brush one's coat.   The atmos-

phere is swarming with evil germs. The objection has been made to Scott that his stories seem unreal. This is scarcely just. History as well as romance speaks in those novels with what Sir Walter himself called the "big bowbow," and their weight of truth will withstand yet a long while the puffs of "scientific" criticism aimed at their "artless loquacity" of style. The lasting underglow of his works is their sturdy spirit of elemental honesty and sympathy with the right.

It may be unfashionable to express art in the simple terms of moral responsibility — the taste of our moment may not relish honesty; but behind the taste lies disease. Certainly if we need filth to feed upon we are in a bad way. Here comes forth the significance of expression; for in art as in a face the countenance is the outer manifestation of inner value. What the Greeks named κατοχή, the enthusiasm of inspiration, may be of good or of evil; but we have a way to distinguish. No paint and powder of mere artifice can make the sweet glow of

health on cheek and lip. Instinctively we know
through some fine ray of expression the pure
from the spurious ; and every thrill of fascination tells us where its wellspring is, and
whether it is good or bad. Beauty is of ethical
importance ; even mere beauty of raiment. Let
whatever is clothed be adorned, not decorated.
A sense of being well dressed is not the same
as a consciousness of wearing foppish finery.
A book, an oration, a poem, a sermon, is but the
measure of a man, and it betrays good or bad
taste in the same way that a man does.

We think aside that it is no strong sign of
greatness for a man to be troubled about the
fashion-plates in the tailor's window ; and I venture to remark that no very great book wears
clothes of the extreme current style. Paris sets
the pace for light people ; but no genuine genius
can be led by the nose ; he likes a way of his
own. So it appears that expression is indeed,
while nominally (or rather conventionally) superficial, the radical characteristic, the innermost
meaning outwardly manifest of organic art.

There is in the word ἦθος a lingering trace of
the earlier definition — the lair of a wild thing —
the gleam of eyes in the gloom of a cave, the independence absolute and resolute of nature lying
on a primitive bed, the στιβάς of the old poets.
The soul of man, in other words, glares out or
smiles out through his style, and expression relates to the conduct of life just as the fluidity of
matter relates to movement ; for culture does
not change substance, but renders it plastic,
malleable, ductile.   Etherealized in the empyrean we have no giddiness in whirling with the
stars ; annealed in the heat of hell we play with
fire and feel no shriveling of conscience.   It is
easy enough to see when a man is dipping his
pen into his ink-pot of culture instead of into
the veins of his being; the outcome is the difference between impression and expression.
The pseudo-realists, like Mr. James, and the
genuine realists, like Paul Bourget, are confess-
edly mere reporters ; consequently, no matter
how analytical in manner, they are in fact but
superficial impressionists.   They pour no wine

of life from within — they express no sap of
originality.   What Jane Austen was in her day
Mr. James and his "school" are to our day — a
cleverly trained and finely modulated voice of
current social gossip.   No amount of analytical
refinement can give to this voice the holding
and haunting power.   So with the true realist,
Paul Bourget, who to-day stands in the old shoes
of the Abbé Prevost ; his novels have only the
strong fascination of evil, the eye of the deadly
serpent.   Are these novels medicine for sick
souls or confections for well ones ?

Let us see-saw this alternative.   Art is for
reform or it is for *delectation* ; there is no Mid-
way Plaisance.   But how shall the mere realistic
reproduction of the social evil, as in a mirror,
work reform to the great mass of honest society ?
Or how can it legitimately delectate a pure mind
or a mind preferring purity ?   Such art is either
a fool's folly or a pander's lure.   It is either
filth for the good, or vice for the vicious.   The
subtlest quality of expression exerts a sort of
electrical influence for good or for bad.   As a

battery current flowing through certain metals disintegrates or molecularly reforms their substance, so the thrill of art, for weal or ill, changes the crystals of the imagination and shocks character into conformity with the noble aspiration or the groveling passion it arouses and feeds. We might take stock of history and find its larger statistics intensely significant in this connection. A loose or reckless moral temper shows in epochs as clearly as in persons. The style, the $\mathring{\eta}\theta o\varsigma$, of a period as it gleams from the record gives the golden key of that civilization. I read a man as I read geology, by the *strata* he has built and the organic forms they inclose. If he has believed on evil he has deposited pessimism. Despite every condition, it is out of his central absolute self-core that man delivers his message; no other order of expression amounts to authentic communication. The ethical concern is to warm and purify the self-core. It is the mission of Christian civilization to make the source of expression pure, so that the face of life shall have an honest and hopeful countenance.

I am mindful of the limitations I must observe; but I will risk suggesting the universal application of what I have but intimated. In our republic we have but one final absolute vehicle of political expression — the ballot. Through it life and all that life can compass are controlled; but if the ballot is a mere commodity on the stalls for sale what becomes of life? Our Senators speak for our States; but if Senators buy their seats or sell their official influence, what is the measure of political expression? Our preachers stand as mouth-pieces of Christianity; but if they find their field only where salary is largest, what is the true exponent of their purpose? And now I offer either horn of the dilemma, — let art be for education, or let it be for comfort or delectation ; in either case to be safe it must be sound and sweet in substance and in essence. But where does it sink to when it assumes the position and condition of mere unconscionable commercial manufacture? At this point the artist stands ready to meet any mood of public debauchery with the tipple it affects.

I thoroughly sympathize with the scientific spirit in the true field of science ; but I cannot conceive of any kinship between the mood of science and the mood of art.   So soon as art is set to academic rule it becomes mere artisanship. Baudelaire proposed to teach the art of poetry just as we teach mathematics ; but no pupil of his ever wrote true poetry.   The only way to control art or religion or political impulse is to educate the taste of the world, for the genius is all men in one ; in almost every instance he comes out of the average class, that middle stratum into which rises the rank sap of low life and upon which settles the richest sediments of all the higher currents. We speak of mud-sills. Well, if the mud-sills are sound, the building has a good base.   Moral education is needed on the ground, among the classes whence genius rises. Let the imagination of the masses be trained in pure channels and taste will take care of itself. Almost every person reads now with a growing appetite for the flavor of art.   Shall the rudimentary lesson of literature for these awakening millions be a discouraging and debauching pessimism? Decadence lies that way. Not mere literary decadence alone; but the breaking up of the heroic tissues of manhood.

I cannot accept art as the dream of irresponsibility, nor yet as the mere photography of visible nature. It must enlarge vision and glorify prospects, not in the fairy-tale mood, but in the mood of faith in God and in mankind. It is not time to discard heroism; what we need is the higher heroism and more heroism. The poet and the novelist may well dream of, nay, awake to examine, a more exalted chivalry than the templars knew, a higher regard for woman, for wifehood, motherhood, manhood, brotherhood, fatherhood. In Paris a pure girl dare not venture in broad daylight alone in the best street. There too is where a novel or a poem nearly always keys itself in illicit love. Glance at the face of Parisian fiction, and you see the countenance of a courtesan. The gleam of evil comes from within. Its expression suggests that no woman is pure, no man honorable, no home free of the scarlet stain. Realism has found this sort of thing fascinating and is beginning to import it into our fiction and poetry for the healing it brings to diseased souls! We may treat lightly the fact that cheap editions of these novels are devoured by our shop-girls, our factory-girls, our poor women everywhere hungry for something to amuse the imagination withal; we may avoid the truth while evading observation; but yet we know what is coming to future generations when our college boys gorge their minds with De Maupassant and Zola and Bourget and Hardy and Flaubert, recommended to them, alas, by the leading critics! I do not care to draw pictures, nor would I appeal by means of mere emphasis of apprehension. It is one thing to recognize genius and it is quite another thing to accept and assimilate the evil that genius does. Flaubert was unquestionably a great genius; but the sort of novels he wrote cannot but carry an evil influence into any mind.

Here then is the ethical connection: what we express by art is the loosing of a fascination which takes hold upon the innermost sources of life to color conduct through a hundred hidden veins. In the countenance of a fiction or a poem we find the magnetism of good or evil out of a genius able to master our imagination and set us forth upon a new way. Rare Ben Jonson touched the key-note of ethics when he said of the poet, "We do not require of him mere elocution, or an excellent faculty in verse, but the exact knowledge of all virtues and their contraries, with ability to render one loved, the other hated, by his proper embattling them." Again he sounds it when he remarks, "Language most shows a man: speak, that I may see thee. . . No glass renders a man's form or likeness so true as his speech." He says that speech is "likened to a man," and that a "good man always profits by his endeavor. . . So good authors in their style." It was Matthew Arnold, a cunning stylist, and in the main a safe critic,

who observed closely, that said of the best English style, it is "magical," contradistinguishing
it from the Greek style. I find true style everywhere magical, and it seems to me that the use
of this magic does not fall outside the bound of
ethics ; that it is a part of the conduct of life
so to direct its use that it shall not become
black magic.

Our scientists are turning their search-lights
upon hypnotism or the alleged mysterious power
of personal physical magnetism. In the expression of genius lurks a force, almost irresistible
and yet more occult than mesmerism, which
may work for ill or for good. But I will discard
genius and take the case of the average literary
artificer, the successful novelist who makes his
bread out of his ink-horn. In no small degree
the literary artist is a sorcerer ; he takes posses-
sion of his reader by a force proportionate to
style. An evil subject may have in itself a fascination, but style will make it irresistible. So
of a good subject. "Virtues and their contraries" are handled by this magic and exhibited for

our good or our harm with all the power of verisimilitude; and the result is the same, whether art is for education or for mere amusement. Here again we are cast back upon the largest consideration of life, that conduct is a seed to-day, a fruit to-morrow, and that what is sown in art produces the food for the thousands whose only share in æsthetic economy is to eat, assimilate, and grow. The banquet may be for pleasure only; but the result is drunkenness or healthful alimentation, a headache or a pleasant memory. It was the burden of heathen song that our individual span of life is all. The merry Greek saw nothing in the long run, thought not of mankind, but only of himself and the space between him and the grave. Our era came in with a teaching which awoke a sense of one generation's responsibility for strains running through all succeeding generations. We cannot escape, try as we may, the tension of the endless chain, of which each of us is an imperishable link.

Speaking my own mind, art seems to me both for education and for rational delectation, and the expression of it demands highest regard for the outcome. We are but children, and whether in schoolroom or play-ground, what we take in becomes a part of us and shines or scowls for evermore in the countenance of character, τὸ ἦθος καὶ τὸ ἄνθος, the flash from within and the bloom of desire.